Monmouthshire's Lost Railways
Peter Dale

Blaina Station.

Acknowledgements

The publishers wish to thank the following for contributing photographs to this book: John Alsop for the front cover, the inside front and back covers, pages 1, 2, 3 (right), 5, 7, 8, 11, 12, 13, 14, 15, 16, 17, 18, 19, 20, 21, 22, 27, 29, 33, 34, 36, 37, 38, 40, 41, 44, 45, 46, 47 and 48; and Richard Casserley for the back cover and pages 3 (left), 4, 6, 9, 23, 24, 25, 26, 28, 30, 31, 32, 35, 39, 42, 43.

Introduction

While parts of Monmouthshire (now in the county of Gwent) are delightfully rural the area around Newport and west into Glamorgan was until fairly recently heavily industrialised with coal mining and steel production. Some of the earliest industrialisation of the area was to do with the smelting of tin and copper. Consequently there were a considerable number of early tramroads or plateways in the area and some of these lines may have carried passengers (see the Sirhowy Valley Line), sometimes unofficially.

The broad gauge South Wales Railway, which was given parliamentary approval in 1846, ran roughly along the coast from Grange Court to Haverfordwest. After it was absorbed by the Great Western Railway in August 1863 that company dominated the county in railway terms. However the London & North Western Railway had a strong presence in the north of the county while two local lines, the Brecon & Merthyr Railway (with its red locomotives and dark chocolate coaches) and the Alexandra Docks Railway, could be found in the Newport area.

A term frequently used through this book is the 'Grouping' and an explanation of its significance is offered for non-railway enthusiasts here. Many of the railways in Britain were built by small companies, sometimes with the backing of a larger company. In the years leading up to 1923 there was a process of consolidation by which smaller companies amalgamated or were absorbed by larger ones but in 1922 there were still well over 100 different railway companies in Britain. In 1923 all but a few minor companies were grouped into four larger concerns by Act of Parliament. They were the Great Western Railway (which continued in an enlarged form), the Southern Railway, the London, Midland & Scottish Railway (which included the London & North Western Railway mentioned above)

and the London & North Eastern Railway. These four companies – often referred to as the 'Big Four' - continued until nationalisation in 1948.

Under British Railways a Modernisation Plan introduced in 1955 spelt the beginning of the end for steam in Britain while the Beeching Plan of 1963 saw the start of widespread closures of many minor, and some major, lines.

Although this book is concerned with passenger railways it should not be forgotten that there was also (and still is to a lesser extent) a large mileage of freight-only lines, not only owned by the railway companies but also by collieries themselves. Some years after main-line steam had finished small tank engines could still be seen doing a real job of work on lines then owned by the National Coal Board.

As the railway lines in the county ultimately fell into the control either of the Great Western Railway or the London & North Western (the London, Midland & Scottish after 1923), this book is arranged giving the Great Western-related lines first (Brecon & Merthyr Tydfill Junction Railway through to the Wye Valley Railway), followed by those related to the London & North Western (the Abersychan Branch through to the Sirhowy Valley Line). The book concludes with a section detailing closed passenger stations on lines remaining open to passenger services.

Trevil Station, 16 July 1959.

Panteg & Griffithstown Station.

Brecon & Merthyr Tydfil Junction Railway

The Brecon & Abergavenny Canal opened in December 1811 but communications from Brecon to the industrial area around Merthyr Tydfil were difficult, there being a high ridge of hills which formed a barrier to transport. The Brecon & Merthyr Tydfil Junction Railway was authorised as far as Talybont in August 1859 with the rest of the line being authorised in 1860 and 1862. However, besides linking the towns of its title (Merthyr having been reached by means of a branch), the line was extended by use of running powers right into Newport. At the Grouping the Brecon & Merthyr became a subsidiary company, rather than a constituent, of the Great Western group.

Brecon & Merthyr Main Line: Southern Division *

Passenger service withdrawn	31 December 1962	*Stations closed*	*Date of closure*
Distance	15.7 miles	Machen	31 December 1962
(Southern Division: Bargoed South Junction to Bassaleg Junction)		Church Road	16 September 1957
Company	Brecon & Merthyr Tydfil Junction Railway /	Rhiwderin	1 March 1954
	Rumney Tramroad	Bassaleg	31 December 1962

Stations closed	*Date of closure*
Pengam (Mon) **	31 December 1962
Fleur-de-Lis Platform	31 December 1962
Maesycwmmer ***	31 December 1962
Bedwas	31 December 1962
Trethomas	31 December 1962

* The Northern Division (Brecon to Deri Junction) lay in Glamorganshire.

** Originally named Pengam; renamed Pengam & Fleur-de-Lis on 1 February 1909; renamed Fleur-de-Lis on 1 July 1924; renamed Pengam (Mon) on 29 March 1926.

*** Renamed as Maesycwmmer & Hengoed on 12 March 1906, reverting back to Maesycwmmer on 1 July 1924.

Fleur-de-Lis Platform, 12 July 1956.

Maesycwmmer Station.

The Rumney Tramroad was authorised in 1825, as a plateway to a gauge of four feet two inches from the Rhymney ironworks to a junction with the Monmouthshire Railway at Bassaleg and ran along the east side of the Rhymney valley. In 1861 the company obtained powers to rebuild the line as a railway but ran into financial problems. At this point the Brecon & Merthyr took the opportunity to purchase the line and use it to extend its own line into Newport. As its line from Brecon came into the western side of the Rhymney valley it obtained running powers over the Rhymney Railway from Deri Junction to Bargoed South Junction, where it left to the eastern side of the valley, a distance of just over 2.5 miles. From Bargoed South Junction it built a line to regain the route of the Rumney Tramroad, and running powers from Bassaleg to Newport – about 2.75 miles – completed the route.

A train to Caerphilly at Machen Station, 13 September 1951.

In 1910 there were only three daily trains between Brecon and Newport, although this increased to four in 1922. One of the more interesting services operated over the line was the through coaches operated from South Wales to Aberystwyth in conjunction with the mid-Wales line of the Cambrian Railways. The Taff Vale's coaches left Cardiff at 10.20 a.m., the Rhymney's left at 10.35 a.m., while the Brecon & Merthyr ran a coach from Newport. From Merthyr they were worked together to Talyllyn South where a Cambrian engine took over, arriving in Aberystwyth at 4.15 p.m.

Brecon & Merthyr Tydfil Junction Railway – Brecon & Merthyr Main Line: Southern Division

Church Road Station.

Brecon & Merthyr: Rhymney Branch

Passenger service withdrawn	Rhymney Lower to New Tredegar:
	14 April 1930
	New Tredegar to Aber Bargoed Junction:
	31 December 1962
Distance	5.8 miles
	(Aber Bargoed Junction to Rhymney)
Company	Brecon & Merthyr Tydfil Junction Railway /
	Rumney Tramroad

Stations closed	*Date of closure*
Rhymney Lower *	14 April 1930
Abertysswg	14 April 1930
McLaren Colliery Platform (for miners)	Unknown
New Tredegar Colliery Platform (for miners)	by July 1930
New Tredegar **	31 December 1962
Elliot Pit Colliery Platform (for miners) ***	31 December 1962
Cwmsyfiog ****	31 December 1962
Cwmsyfiog Colliery Halt (for miners) †	31 December 1962
Aberbargoed ††	31 December 1962

* Originally named Rhymney; renamed Rhymney & Pontlottyn on 1 September 1905; renamed as Rhymney Pwll Uchaf on 1 July 1924; renamed Rhymney Lower on 17 September 1926.

** Originally named White Rose; renamed New Tredegar & Whiterose on 1 July 1885; renamed New Tredegar & Tirphil on 1 November 1906; renamed New Tredegar on 1 July 1924.

*** Earlier named Elliot Pit Colliery Halt (open by 1909).

**** Replaced the first Cwmsyfiog Station, which was 585 metres south, on 1 July 1937.

† Originally named Cwmsyfiog & Brithdir; renamed Cwmsyfiog on 1 July 1924 and closed on 5 July 1937; reopened as Cwmsyfiog Colliery Halt on 6 December 1937.

†† Originally named Aber Bargoed, closing in October 1869; reopened in March 1870 and renamed Aber Bargoed & Bargoed on 1 September 1905; renamed Bargoed & Aberbargoed on 1 March 1909, becoming Aberbargoed on 1 July 1924.

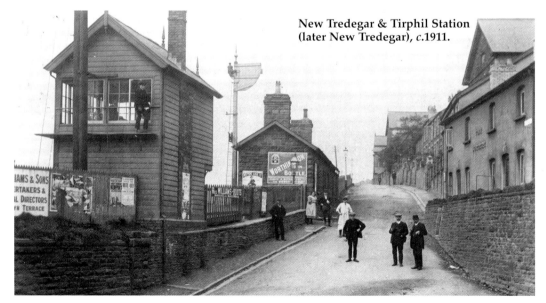

New Tredegar & Tirphil Station (later New Tredegar), *c.*1911.

Locomotive No. 9488 approaches Cwmsyfiog Station with a service from New Tredegar to Newport, 13 October 1962.

When the Brecon & Merthyr Junction Railway bought the Rumney Tramroad it not only acquired a route to Newport but the old tramroad line to Rhymney and the lucrative traffic on it. The line reopened as a railway to Rhymney on 16 April 1866 and was double track except for the last section between Abertysswg and Rhymney. During the summer of 1916 there was a landslide which blocked one track and another landslide in April 1930 brought about the permanent closure of the line above New Tredegar.

In 1910 there were five daily services and an additional one on Saturday. In 1922 this had grown to six daily trains and two more on Saturday, most trains running to and from Newport.

Bristol & South Wales Union Railway

Passenger service withdrawn	1 December 1886
Distance	0.9 miles
Company	Bristol & South Wales Union Railway

Stations closed	*Date of closure*
Portskewett Pier *	1 December 1886

* Closed between 23 May and 15 June 1881.

This line ran from Bristol to New Passage (about 11.5 miles) in Gloucestershire with a ferry across to Portskewett Pier from where a junction was made with the South Wales main line. Although the tide here can vary by as much as 46 feet a system of stairs and lifts to pontoons beside the piers enabled the ferry to moor whatever the state of the tide. The line opened on 1 January 1864 and was worked by the Great Western. It closed when the Severn Tunnel opened in 1886.

Hall's Tramroad

Passenger service withdrawn	25 September 1939
Distance	3.8 miles (Penar Junction to Manmoel Colliery)
Company	Great Western Railway

Stations closed	*Date of closure*
Oakdale Halt *	12 September 1932
Penmaen Halt	25 September 1939

* Originally known as Penmawr & Oakdale Halt, date of change unknown.

This line had its origin as one of the tramroads that fed into the Monmouthshire railway system and ran from the Western Valley Railway lines near Cross Keys to collieries at Manmoel. When the London & North Western Railway took over the Sirhowy line the Great Western Railway wanted to obtain an independent route from Aberdare to Newport and so entered into a 1,000-year lease of Hall's Tramroad in October 1877 with a view to upgrading it to a railway. Nothing was done in the short term as agreement had been reached with the London & North Western to allow Great Western trains to continue running over the Sirhowy line. Colliery development in the north Sirhowy Valley led to the opening of the section north of Penar Junction on the Taff Vale Extension line to Manmoel Colliery on 10 March 1886. The southern section did not open until 1912, but as the northern part was the only one to carry a passenger service that is what interests us here. The passenger service did not begin until 14 March 1927 with an auto-train service between Crumlin, Pontypool Road and Penmaen & Oakdale halts. By 1938 there was a passenger service only on a Friday, one train to and from Pontypool Road and two to and from Crumlin High Level.

Monmouthshire Railway

The Monmouthshire Canal Company obtained an Act in 1792 to build canals linking Newport to industries inland. The company was also empowered to build linking tramroads, notably that to Blaenavon and, north of Crumlin, to Nantyglo. It was also given wide-ranging powers to build rail or waggonways from its lines to any ironworks, limestone quarries or coalmines within eight miles. Likewise, powers were given to the owners of coalmines to build lines should the canal refuse to build them.

This resulted in two canals, linked just north of Newport, and associated tramroads known as the Western Valleys (to Risca and Beaufort) and the Eastern Valleys (to Pontypool and Blaenavon). In 1802 a further Act allowed the construction of a line from Nine Mile Point to the canal near Newport. This brought about the anomaly of the Park Mile whereby the portion of the line that passed through Tredegar Park (about a mile) remained the property of the Morgan family, who received tolls over that section and had to maintain it (a situation which continued until the section was bought by the Great Western Railway on 1 January 1923). At the same time powers were granted to build a railway parallel to the canal from this line to the Monmouthshire's line at Crumlin. The Sirhowy Tramroad was incorporated by the same Act to build its line from Nine Mile Point to the Sirhowy Furnaces. Passenger service on these lines began in 1822, provided by John Kingson of Newport in a vehicle known as the 'caravan'. The first use of a locomotive on the lines was in December 1829. The company was very prosperous, returning over 10% profits for 28 years from 1819.

However, many of its customers regarded it as a restrictive monopoly with high prices and a poorly maintained track. Dissatisfaction was so strong that a rival railway was proposed in 1843. As a result of this, in 1845, the Monmouthshire applied for powers to improve its system, make a new railway from Newport to Pontypool and operate the traffic themselves (previously customers had provided their own waggons and paid tolls). At this time the company had $21\frac{1}{2}$ miles of canal, 30 of tramroads and 10 of railroads. In the Western Valleys an additional $72\frac{1}{2}$ miles of tramroads owned by other companies joined the Monmouthshire. The conversion and improvements did not go smoothly and although the Act required the work to be complete in three years further Acts were required to complete the work. Much later the Western Valley lines and Eastern Valley lines were to come together again at Brynmawr on the Heads of Valleys line.

The Monmouthshire flirted with a number of other companies, including the London & North Western Railway which had running powers over it into Newport and ran a passenger service into the town's Mill Street until the end of 1865. There was another affair with the Midland Railway to acquire jointly the Brecon & Merthyr Railway, although this was dropped when the Midland withdrew. Much Monmouthshire traffic came by carrying Great Western trains between Pontypool and Newport on the Eastern section, but when the Great Western's own line from Pontypool to Newport opened in 1874 this traffic was lost. A further source of Great Western traffic between Nine Mile Point and Waterloo Junction (Newport) on the Western Valleys section was at risk when the Great Western obtained authority in 1875 for a line between Caerleon and Nine Mile Point, effectively by-passing Newport. The Monmouthshire then reached agreement for the Great Western to lease the entire system from 1 August 1875 followed by amalgamation in August 1880.

Abertillery Station, *c.*1915.

Western Valley Lines: Newport to Brynmawr

Passenger service withdrawn	30 April 1962 (Brynmawr to Bassaleg Junction)
	31 December 1962 (Bassaleg Junction to Gaer Junction)
Distance	22.8 miles
Company	Monmouthshire Railway /
	Great Western Railway / London & North Western Railway

Stations closed	*Date of closure*
Nantyglo	30 April 1962
Blaina	30 April 1962
Bournville Halt *	30 April 1962
Abertillery **	30 April 1962
Six Bells Halt	30 April 1962
Aberbeeg	30 April 1962
Llanhilleth	30 April 1962
Crumlin Low Level ***	30 April 1962
Newbridge	30 April 1962
Abercarn	30 April 1962

Stations closed	*Date of closure*
Cross Keys	30 April 1962
Risca ****	30 April 1962
Rogerstone *****	30 April 1962
Bassaleg Junction †	30 April 1962
Newport Court-y-bella ††	4 August 1852
Newport Dock Street	11 March 1880

* Originally named Tylers (or Tylors) Arms Platform until 30 October 1933.
** This station replaced an earlier one to the south in 1893.
*** Originally named Crumlin until 1 September 1881.
**** Sometimes known as Risca for Pontymister.
***** Originally named Tydu until 20 October 1898.
† Originally named Bassaleg until 1 July 1924. Closed between 1 January 1917 and 1 March 1919.
†† This was a temporary station used prior to the opening of Dock Street.

Aberbeeg Station.

Llanhilleth Station.

The tramroad passenger service to Blaina was started on 21 December 1850 and Dock Street Station opened on 4 August 1852. Conversion of the Western Valley lines from tramroads to railways was not complete until May 1855 (although the Nine Mile Point branch was still not ready by that point). Until then Newport had three stations served by lines of three different gauges – High Street: broad gauge, Mill Street: standard, Dock Street: 4ft 4 inch. The line was extended from Blaina to Nantyglo in 1858.

Crumlin Low Level Station.

A loop allowing Western Valleys trains access to the South Wales main line opened in January 1879. On 11 March 1880 a rebuilt and enlarged High Street Station opened after which all Newport passengers, including those of the London & North Western and the Brecon & Merthyr, used this station. On 28 May 1906 the extension to Brynmawr was opened (Brynmawr & Western Valleys Railway) jointly with the London & North Western.

Newbridge Station, *c*.1915.

Western Valley Lines: Ebbw Vale Branch

Passenger service withdrawn	30 April 1962
Distance	6.7 miles (Aberbeeg to Ebbw Vale)
Company	Monmouthshire Railway

Stations closed	*Date of closure*
Ebbw Vale Low Level *	30 April 1962
Victoria	30 April 1962
Cwm	30 April 1962

* Originally named as Ebbw Vale until 19 July 1950.

Locomotive No. 3798 with the 9.15 a.m. service to newport at Ebbw Vale Low Level Station, 12 July 1958. The passenger service to Ebbw Vale began on 19 April 1852.

Cwm Station, *c.*1915.

Western Valley Lines: Nine Mile Point Branch *

Passenger service withdrawn	13 June 1960
Distance	2.3 miles (Risca to Nine Mile Point)
Company	Monmouthshire Railway

* There were no stations on this section.

The Nine Mile Point branch was rebuilt as a railway by November 1855 but was not used by passengers until the Sirhowy Railway opened in June 1865 (see Heads of the Valleys line).

Eastern Valley Lines: Newport — Blaenavon

Passenger service withdrawn	30 April 1962 (Blaenavon Low Level to Pontypool)
Distance	16.3 miles
Company	Monmouthshire Railway

Stations closed	*Date of closure*
Blaenavon Low Level *	30 April 1962
Cwmavon Halt **	30 April 1962
Cwmffrwd Halt	30 April 1962
Abersychan Low Level ***	30 April 1962
Snatchwood Halt	5 October 1953
Pontnewydd	30 April 1962
Pontypool Crane Street	30 April 1962
Pontypool Blaendare Road Halt	30 April 1962
Panteg & Griffithstown ****	30 April 1962
Sebastopol	30 April 1962
Pontrhydyrun †	30 April 1962
Upper Pontnewydd ††	30 April 1962
Cwmbran †††	11 March 1880

Stations closed	*Date of closure*
Llantarnam	11 March 1880
Marshes Turnpike Gate	9 March 1853
Newport Mill Street	11 March 1880

* Originally named Blaenavon until 19 July 1950.

** Originally named Cwmavon until 1 January 1902; renamed Cwmavon (Mons) until 8 June 1953.

*** Originally named Abersychan until 14 May 1885.

**** Originally named Panteg until 1898, the station opened in July 1880 having replaced an earlier station of the same name. That station was known as Sebastopol until January 1875.

† Closed 1 January 1917 and opened as Pontrhydyrun Halt in July 1933.

†† Known as Upper Cwmbran only between 1 September and 4 November 1881. Prior to that known as Pontnewydd.

††† A new station on the Pontypool Caerleon and Newport line replaced this station.

Abersychan Low level Station, *c.*1916.

The line to Pontypool was authorised by the 1845 Act as a standard gauge line from Newport to the point where the Blaenavon Railroad began. After financial difficulties the line opened on 1 July 1852 from a temporary terminus at Marshes Turnpike Gate. The extension into Mill Street opened in March 1853. In June 1854 it was extended to join the Blaenavon which had been converted to a standard gauge railway a year earlier. Passenger trains started to run through to Blaenavon on 2 October 1854. When the enlarged Newport High Street Station was opened on 11 March 1880 passenger trains were diverted over the Pontypool, Caerleon and Newport line south of Cwmbran.

Cwmbran Station.

Eastern Valley Lines: Talywain Branch

Passenger service withdrawn	5 May 1941
Distance	2 miles (Abersychan to Pontypool Crane Street)
Company	Monmouthshire Railway

Stations closed	*Date of closure*
Pentwyn Halt	5 May 1941
Pentrepiod Halt	5 May 1941
Cwmffrwdoer Halt	5 May 1941
Waenfelin Halt *	5 May 1941

* Closed between 30 April 1917 and 30 April 1928.

The Talywain branch was completed in September 1879 and through trains started to run from Newport and on to the London & North Western branch from Brynmawr. Services finished on this line on the same date as the ex-London & North Western branch.

Coleford, Monmouth, Usk & Pontypool Railway

Passenger service withdrawn   30 May 1955
Distance   16.5 miles (Little Mill Junction to Monmouth Troy)
Company   Coleford, Monmouth, Usk & Pontypool Railway

Stations closed	*Date of closure*
Little Mill Junction *	30 May 1955
Glascoed Halt	30 May 1955
Usk	30 May 1955
Cefn Tilla Halt	30 May 1955
Llandenny	30 May 1955
Raglan Road Crossing	30 May 1955
Raglan **	30 May 1955

Stations closed	*Date of closure*
Elms Bridge Halt	30 May 1955
Dingestow	30 May 1955
Monmouth Troy ***	5 January 1959

* Originally named Little Mill until 1 July 1883. Closed by the West Midland Railway in July 1861 and reopened in May 1883.

** Originally named Raglan Footpath until 1 July 1876. There is a reference to another station nearby known as Raglan Road which closed on 1 July 1876.

*** This station got its unusual name from its proximity to the neighbouring Troy House and the River Trothy.

Usk Station, 11 April 1955.

Cefn Tilla Halt, 11 April 1955.

The Coleford, Monmouth, Usk & Pontypool Railway was authorised in August 1853 with powers to also take over the Monmouth Railway. It opened as far as Usk on 2 June 1856 and on to Monmouth on 12 October 1857. It was worked by the Newport, Abergavenny & Hereford Railway until it opened to Monmouth, after which the owning company worked it themselves using two locomotives hired from the NA&H. An extension over the River Wye to Wyesham, where it connected with the Monmouth company's tramroad, opened in July 1861. In July 1861 the line was leased to the West Midland Railway. The West Midland was absorbed by the Great Western on 1 August 1863 and the CMU&P became part of the Great Western in August 1881.

Coleford, Monmouth, Usk & Pontypool Railway

Locomotive No. 5414 with the 11.50 a.m. service to Chepstow at Monmouth Troy Station, 15 September 1956.

　　Coleford, Monmouth, Usk & Pontypool Railway

Ross & Monmouth Railway *

Passenger service withdrawn	5 January 1959
Distance	13.1 miles (Ross to Monmouth Troy)
Company	Ross & Monmouth Railway

Stations closed	*Date of closure*
Hadnock Halt	5 January 1959
Monmouth May Hill	5 January 1959

* The closed stations on this line that were in Herefordshire were Ross-On-Wye and Kerne Bridge. The closed stations in Gloucestershire were Lydbrook Junction and Symond's Yat.

A flooded Monmouth May Hill Station.

The Ross & Monmouth Railway was authorised in July 1865 and opened to Monmouth May Hill on 4 August 1873. It was worked from the outset by the Great Western which opened the extension to Monmouth Troy on 1 May 1874. After the connection into Monmouth Troy was made many of the trains worked as through services from Ross to Pontypool Road. The R&M was not absorbed by the Great Western until 1922 when the service comprised five trains daily in each direction, of which four started from or terminated at Pontypool Road, with an additional service on Thursdays and Saturdays. As was often the case there was no Sunday service.

By 1952 there were still five trains daily and autotrains were running the service. Although it was a very scenic line that was not enough to justify its retention; after the withdrawal of passenger services goods services continued to Lydbrook Junction until November 1964 and even then private siding traffic continued until November the following year.

Taff Vale Extension Railway *

Passenger service withdrawn	15 June 1964	
Distance	20.8 miles (Pontypool to Middle Duffryn)	
Company	Newport, Abergavenny & Hereford Railway	

Stations closed	*Date of closure*
Pontypool Clarence Street **	15 June 1964
Cefn Crib	October 1860
Crumlin Valley Colliery Platform (for miners)	6 November 1961
Hafodyrynys Platform	15 June 1964
Crumlin ***	1 June 1857
Crumlin High Level ****	15 June 1964
Treowen Halt	11 July 1960
Pentwynmawr Platform	15 June 1964
Penar Junction Halt	1 January 1917
Pontllanfraith Low Level †	15 June 1964

* The closed stations on this line that were in Glamorganshire were Hengoed High Level, Llancaiach, Nelson & Llancaiach, Treharris, Trelewis Halt, Quaker's Yard High Level, Penrhiwceiber High Level, Mountain Ash Cardiff Road and Duffryn Crossin Halt.

** Originally named Pontypool; renamed Pontypool Town on April 1867; renamed Pontypool Clarence Street on 1 September 1881.

*** This was a temporary station which was replaced by Crumlin for Western Valley when the Crumlin Viaduct opened.

**** Named Crumlin for Western Valley until 1 September 1881.

† Originally named Tredegar Junction; renamed Pontllanfraith on 1 May 1905; renamed Pontllanfraith Low Level on 19 July 1950.

The Taff Vale Extension Railway of the Newport, Abergavenny & Hereford Railway was authorised as a standard gauge line in 1846. It ran from Pontypool Road to a junction with the Taff Vale Railway at Quaker's Yard. Once the Crumlin Viaduct (at 1,650 feet long and a maximum height of 200 feet, the largest in the world at the time) was ready it opened as far as Pontllanfraith on 1 June 1857 and on to Quaker's Yard Low Level on 11 January 1858, where it provided the Taff Vale Railway with its first link to another railway of the same gauge so that Quaker's Yard became a very busy interchange point.

Parliamentary approval for an extension to link with the Vale of Neath Railway at Middle Duffryn was obtained in 1857 but in case the Neath line retained the broad gauge it also gained powers to join the Taff Vale at Mountain Ash and use its lines to Aberdare. The extension did not open for freight until January 1864 and passengers in October of the same year. The NA&H became part of the West Midland Railway when that company was formed on 14 June 1860; the West Midland was itself absorbed by the Great Western on 1 August 1863.

Pontllanfraith Low Level Station, 10 July 1958.

Wye Valley Railway *

Passenger service withdrawn	5 January 1959	*Stations closed*	*Date of closure*
Distance	13.1 miles	Penallt	5 January 1959
Company	Wye Valley Railway	Wyesham Halt	5 January 1959

Stations closed	*Date of closure*
Tintern **	5 January 1959
Brockweir	5 January 1959
Llandogo Halt	5 January 1959
St Briavels ***	5 January 1959
Whitebrook Halt	5 January 1959

* Closed stations on this line that were in Gloucestershire were Tidenham, Netherhope and Redbrook-on-Wye.

** Known as Tintern for Brockweir from sometime in 1912 until 23 September 1923 when it reverted to Tintern.

*** Originally named St Briavels and Llandogo until 9 March 1927.

Tintern station.

Llandogo Halt, 15 September 1956.

The Wye Valley Railway obtained its Act in August 1866. There was considerable delay in commencing construction due to difficulties in raising the necessary finance, the bubble having just burst on the last of the Railway manias. Work began in May 1874 and the line opened from a junction near Chepstow on the South Wales Railway to a junction with the Coleford, Monmouth, Usk & Pontypool Railway at Wyesham Junction (Monmouth) on 1 November 1876. The railway was worked and leased by the Great Western which took it over in 1905.

By the late 1920s traffic was being lost to road competition and here, as on many other lines, the Great Western attempted to win back custom by opening new halts. Between 1927 and 1931 halts were opened at Brockweir, Llandogo, Whitebrook, Penallt, Wyesham and Netherhope while costs were reduced by using autotrains. It did no good and by 1958 the line was losing more than £20,000 per year. In 1922 there were four trains each way daily, with one short working to and from Tintern, all running to and from Severn Tunnel Junction. As usual there was no Sunday service. For much of its life the line was worked by 64xx pannier tanks or 14xx auto tanks working with autotrailers but as early as the 1940s dieselisation began, using the early Great Western railcars. After passenger services ceased goods traffic continued until January 1964. Tintern Station is now a recreational centre, retaining much of its railway past.

Abersychan Branch

Passenger service withdrawn	5 May 1941	*Stations closed*	*Date of closure*
Distance	8.3 miles (Brynmawr to Abersychan)	Blaenavon	5 May 1941
Company	Brynmawr & Blaenavon Railway /	Varteg Halt *	5 May 1941
	London & North Western Railway	Garndiffaith Halt **	5 May 1941
		Abersychan & Talywain	5 May 1941

Stations closed	*Date of closure*	
Waenavon	5 May 1941	* Originally named Varteg until 1933.
Garn-Yr-Erw Halt	5 May 1941	**Originally named Six Bells Halt until 2 October 1922.

Blaenavon Station, 14 July 1958.

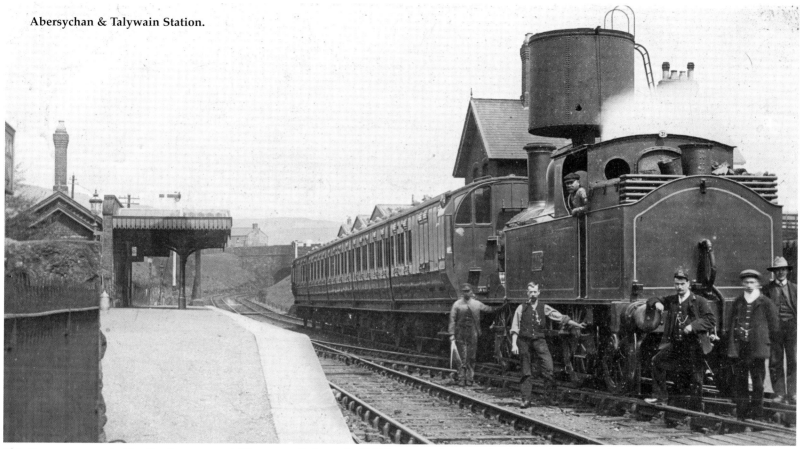

Abersychan & Talywain Station.

This line was promoted by the Brynmawr & Blaenavon Railway in 1866 but was taken over by the London & North Western in the same year. The line opened to Blaenavon in 1869 and in 1877 was extended 3.8 miles to join the Monmouthshire Railway's Cwmfrwyd line (opening on 1 May 1878). At the same time a mineral spur was built to Varteg Hill Colliery. The section through Abersychan Station and a short distance westwards was a joint line. When the Monmouthshire opened a new line connecting to the Cwmfrwyd line a Great Western passenger service was run from Newport to Abersychan and an agreement was reached to extend these trains to Brynmawr, replacing most of the London & North Western workings.

In 1887 there were three trains daily through to Newport and only two as far as Abersychan. By 1922 there was only one through train from Brynmawr to Newport, the others requiring passengers to change trains at Pontpool (Crane Street). Waenavon, at 1,400 feet, was the highest point on the London & North Western system.

EbbwVale Branch

Passenger service withdrawn	5 February 1951
Distance	1.5 miles
Company	London & North Western Railway

Stations closed	*Date of closure*
Ebbw Vale High Level *	5 February 1951

* Originally named Ebbw Vale until renamed on 23 May 1949.

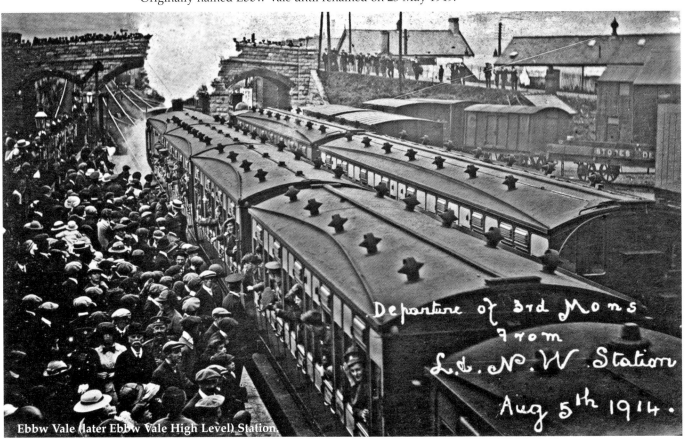

Ebbw Vale (later Ebbw Vale High Level) Station.

This line was built from a junction with the Heads of Valleys line at Beaufort and opened for passengers on 1 September 1867, with goods traffic following at the end of October that year. Generally, trains worked through from Brynmawr and by 1922 there were 15 trains daily taking 10 to 12 minutes for the 3.5-mile journey. There was a gradient of 1 in 42 down to Ebbw Vale and the line was the scene of a spectacular accident in 1910 when a coal train, in the charge of a 0-6-2T, ran away and was wrecked in the station yard, fortunately without serious casualties.

Heads of the Valleys Line *

Passenger service withdrawn	6 January 1958
Distance	24.5 miles (Abergavenny Junction to Merthyr High Street)
Company	Merthyr, Tredegar & Abergavenny Railway

Stations closed	*Date of closure*
Abergavenny Brecon Road	6 January 1958
Govilon	6 January 1958
Beaufort	6 January 1958

Stations closed	*Date of closure*
Trevil	6 January 1958
Nantybwch **	13 June 1960

* The closed stations on this line that were in Brecknockshire were Gilwern Halt, Clydach, Gelli Felen Halt and Brynmawr. The closed stations in Glamorganshire were Rhymney Bridge, Dowlais High Street, Pontsarn and Cefn Coed.

** Originally named Tredegar (Nantybwch) until renamed on 1 November 1868.

Abergavenny Brecon Road Station, *c*.1915.

There were a number of tramroads extending westwards from the Brecon and Abergavenny Canal and one of these, Bailey's Tramroad, built to the unusual gauge of 4 feet 4 inches, formed the basis of the Merthyr, Tredegar & Abergavenny Railway. That scheme had succeeded over the rival Breconshire Railway & Canal Company and was authorised in August 1859. The same Act transferred to the MT&A the section of the 3 feet 6 inch gauge Llanvihangel Railway between the canal wharf at Govilon and the intended junction with the Newport, Abergavenny & Hereford Railway east of Abergavenny.

Beaufort Station.

The line formed an important part of London & North Western Railway strategy to gain access to South Wales industries. Having failed to gain outright control of the NA&H or the Shrewsbury & Hereford Railway, the London & North Western, by being joint lessees of the S&H, was left with running powers over the NA&H and so gained access to Abergavenny. Before the MT&A was opened the London & North Western reached an agreement to lease the line for 1,000 years in the face of opposition from the West Midland Railway. The London & North Western absorbed the MT&A on 30 June 1866. Passenger services began as far as Brynmawr on 1 October 1862 (although this was preceded by a ceremonial opening on 29 September). The line was extended as far as Nantybwch on 1 March 1864. Despite strong opposition from the Brecon & Merthyr Railway the line was extended jointly with the Rhymney Railway to Rhymney Bridge on 5 September 1871 and opened on 1 January 1873 to Ivor Junction with the Brecon & Merthyr's Dowlais line. Access to Merthyr was gained over the B&M Merthyr branch, which had opened in 1868, and became a joint line when the London & North Western paid half the construction cost. The final expensive link between Penywern Junction and Morlais Junction, which included the 574-yard-long Morlais tunnel, was opened on 1 June 1879.

The line was doubled in 1877 and the London & North Western gained access to Cardiff by running powers over the Rhymney Railway. Goods traffic developed so much that the London & North Western opened its own goods depot in the Cardiff Docks district while through coaches were run between Cardiff and Crewe, and Manchester and Liverpool. These through services lasted until the First World War. The onset of the Great Depression brought a rationalisation of goods services with the Great Western and the London Midland & Scottish (which took over the London & North Western) working more closely. LMS goods traffic for Cardiff was sent via Newport so removing the need to work it along the steep gradients of the MT&A. Amongst other steep gradients along the route was over five miles at 1 in 37 to 40 between Govilon and Brynmawr. Remaining goods services were withdrawn on 22 November 1954.

For many years the line was the haunt of London & North Western 0-6-2Ts (Coal Tanks) and almost 50 of them were shedded at Abergavenny, but freight services were worked by Beames 0-8-4Ts and later by 0-8-0s. In the 1950s various Great Western tanks worked the line as it became part of British Railway's Western Region at Nationalisation.

Sirhowy Valley Line

Passenger service withdrawn	13 June 1960	*Stations closed*	*Date of closure*
Distance	15.5 miles (Nantybwch to Nine Mile Point)	Pont Lawrence	4 February 1957
Company	Sirhowy Tramroad / London & North Western Railway	Nine Mile Point	2 February 1959

Stations closed	*Date of closure*
Sirhowy *	13 June 1960
Tredegar *	13 June 1960
Bedwellty Pits Halt *†	13 June 1960
Holly Bush ††	13 June 1960
Markham Village Halt †††	13 June 1960
Argoed Halt ††††	13 June 1960
Blackwood ‡	13 June 1960
Pontllanfraith High Level ‡‡	13 June 1960
Wyllie Halt	13 June 1960
Ynysddu *	13 June 1960

* Closed c.1855 and reopened on 19 June 1865.
† Originally named Bedwellty Pits until renamed on 30 September 1935.
†† Originally named Hollybush until 1 December 1899, it replaced the earlier Sirhowy Tramway station to the north (closed c.1855).
††† Originally named Markham Village until 5 May 1941.
†††† This station replaced the earlier Sirhowy Tramway station (closed c.1855) and was originally named Argoed until 29 September 1941.
‡ Replaced the earlier Sirhowy Tramway station (closed c.1855).
‡‡ Originally named Tredegar Junction until 1 July 1911; renamed Pontllanfraith until 23 May 1949.

Tredegar Station, c.1912.

Argoed Station (later Halt).

This line had its origins in the Sirhowy Tramroad which was authorised in 1802, as part of the Monmouthshire Canal Act, to build a line from Tredegar Iron Works to the Monmouthshire Canal line from Newport (built under the same Act) near Nine Mile Point. It probably opened about 1804 as a plateway to a gauge of 4 feet 2 inches, and was horse worked as a toll road, meaning that carriers had to pay to run waggons over the line. It was extremely successful (returning profits of 18% at one time) and is believed to have influenced the decision of the Stockton & Darlington promoters to build a railway rather than a canal. Horsedrawn passenger traffic began in 1822 and steam locomotives were introduced from 1829.

Blackwood Station, 12 July 1959.

Locomotive 9644 leaving Pontllanfraith High Level Station with a service from Tredegar to Newport, 10 July 1958.

Powers were obtained to convert the line entirely to locomotive working and at the same time the company took over the operation of the line. The line was converted to a modern railway by an Act of May 1860 when the name was changed to the Sirhowy Railway Company. The extension northwards to the London & North Western line at Nantybwch was built under powers granted by Act of June 1865. When passenger trains resumed they ran through to Newport. The connection northwards came into use for goods on 12 October 1868 and for passengers on 2 November.

Nine Mile Point Station, 1939.

In the mid 1870s there was much talk of takeover of the Sirhowy with the Great Western, the Monmouthshire and even the Midland railways being talked of as possible suitors. In the end the Sirhowy went to the London & North Western, being taken over in August 1875. In 1910 there were eight daily services of which six ran through to Newport. For much of its life the line was operated by London & North Western 0-8-4Ts on freight services and Coal Tanks on passenger services. Although official closure was on 13 June 1960, the last train actually ran on 11 June as there was no Sunday service.

Stations closed on lines still open to passengers
Newport — Abergavenny

Stations closed	Date
Caerleon	30 April 1962
Ponthir	30 April 1962
Llantarnam	30 April 1962
Lower Pontnewydd *	9 June 1958
Pontypool Road **	1 March 1909
Nantyderry	9 June 1958
Penpergwm	9 June 1958
Abergavenny Junction ***	9 June 1958
Llanvair	1 October 1854
Llanvihangel (Mon) ****	9 June 1958
Pandy	9 June 1958

* Originally named Pontnewydd until 1 July 1925, closed between 1 January 1917 and 1 May 1919.

** Replaced by a second station, of the same name, about 400 yards to the north.

*** Replaced an earlier station of the same name about 500 yards to the south on 20 June 1870.

**** Originally named Llanvihangel until 10 December 1910; renamed Llanfihangel until 1 January 1900.

Pontypool Road Station. This locomotive was called *Mafeking*.

Nantyderry Station, *c.*1908.

Newport — Abergavenny

South Wales Main Line

Stations closed	Date	Stations closed	Date
Portskewett *	2 November 1964	Ebbw Junction	12 November 1918
Sudbrook	13 August 1978	Marshfield	10 August 1959
Undy Halt	2 November 1964	Roath	2 April 1917
Magor	2 November 1964		
Llanwern	12 September 1960	* Replaced an earlier station about 800 yards to the west on 1 October 1863.	

Portskewett Station, *c.*1913.